Understanding Copyright:

Author's Edition

Understanding Copyright: Author's Edition

Teresa Lynn

Tranquility Press 2019

Understanding Copyright: Author's Edition
© Teresa Lynn 2019 All rights reserved

For information:
Tranquility Press
TranquilityPress.com
723 W University Ave
#300-234
Georgetown TX 78626

Paperback ISBN: 978-1-950481-12-5
e-book ISBN: 978-1-950481-11-8

Library of Congress Control Number:2019947682

Library of Congress Cataloging-in-Publication Data

Names: Lynn, Teresa, 1969- author
Title: Understanding copyright : authors edition / Teresa Lynn
Description: | Austin, Texas : Tranquility Press, 2019 | Includes bibliographical references
Identifiers: LCCN 2019947682 (print) |
ISBN 978-1-950481-12-5 (print) | 978-1-950481-11-8 (e-book)
Subjects: LCSH: Copyright—United States.
Classification: LCC KF2995 | LCC KF3020 |
DDC 346.7304/82-dc23

Contents

Note from the Author

I am not an attorney. I am a writer, an editor, and a publisher.

In each of these capacities, I often run into issues dealing with copyright. Misunderstandings about this topic abound. I've spent many hours reading copyright law, studying guidelines from the US Copyright Office, and consulting with attorneys to keep both myself and my clients from running afoul of the law.

The purpose of this book is to share some educational information on the issues that arise most often for writers. It is not, and should not be considered or taken as, legal advice.

Please note that while every effort has been made toward accuracy, laws—including those dealing with copyright—are subject to change at any time;

and they often do. Therefore, always seek the advice of an attorney specializing in intellectual property regarding any specific questions about your own work.

Teresa Lynn
August 2019

Chapter 1

What Is Copyright?

Although we speak of copyright in the singular, that is misleading. Copyright is actually several separate rights, bundled together and treated as one. Each of these rights is exclusive to the holder, or owner, of the copyright.

The rights included in copyright are:

1) to reproduce the copyrighted work;

2) to prepare derivative works based upon the copyrighted work;

3) to distribute copies of the copyrighted work to the public for compensation or by transfer of ownership;

4) to perform the copyrighted work publicly;

5) to display the copyrighted work publicly; and

6) in the case of sound recordings, to perform

the copyrighted work publicly by means of a digital audio transmission.

Let's examine each of these rights individually.

Right to Reproduce

When discussing copyright, the right to reproduce is often the one that first comes to mind. Reproducing means duplicating or copying by any method, including manually, mechanically, electronically or digitally.

Everyday Application

Saving a photo or meme you find online and then posting it on your social media is a form of reproducing. Since that's a right reserved to the copyright owner, it shouldn't be done without permission.

Right to Prepare Derivatives

Next is the right to prepare derivative works. A derivative work is created by transforming some aspect of one or more existing works to create a new form of the work. To qualify as a derivative work under the law, the new work must use a "substantial" amount of the preexisting work. This means the new work must contain enough of the preexisting work that an average person would recognize that it was adapted from the previous work. There are several ways this right could be exercised by writers: adapting a book into a screenplay or play; translating a book into another language; making an audio recording of a book; and preparing an annotated, abridged, or expanded edition are a few examples.

Everyday Application

Recording yourself reading a book or videoing the illustrations in a picture book to post on your blog is preparing a derivative work. In each case, one form of the work—written—has been transformed into another form—electronically recorded. Since that's a right reserved to the holder of the copyright, it shouldn't be done without permission.

Right to Distribute

The third right in the bundle of copyrights is distribution. It may initially seem that this right is limited by the phrase "for compensation or by transfer of ownership." Some people conclude that as long as they don't take money or other compensation, they can give away copyrighted materials. But the definition of "distribution" is "apportion, scatter, or give out."

It would be extremely difficult, if not impossible, to "give out" a thing, even for free, without that thing becoming the possession of the one who receives it. A change in ownership is inherent in distribution. That change in ownership keeps this right broad.

Right to Publicly Perform

The right to publicly perform a work (the fourth right), including by means of a digital audio transmission (the sixth right), is also reserved to a copyright holder. There are two matters to consider in this right: what it means to "perform," and what "publicly" means.

The law defines "to perform" as "to recite, render, play, dance, or act it, either directly or by means of any device or process or, in the case of a motion picture or other audiovisual work, to show its images in any sequence or to make the sounds accompanying it audible." It seems that any way one can present a work to others is covered under this definition.

"Publicly" has two definitions within copyright law. The first deals with physical places: "at a place open to the public or at any place where a substantial number of persons outside of a normal circle of a family and its social acquaintances is gathered."

The second definition deals with methods: "by means of any device or process, whether the members of the public capable of receiving the performance or display receive it in the same place or in separate places and at the same time or at different times."

Everyday Application

If your daughter and her friends act out a scene from *Little House on the Prairie* and invite the entire community to watch, they could be criticized (or worse) for "publicly performing."

But if your son makes a recording of himself reciting lines from a *Harry Potter* book and emails it to his father overseas, his performance is not "public," so he's probably safe.

However, if he puts the video on Twitter and tells his father to look at it there, he has made the video public.

Right to Display

Finally, the copyright owner reserves the right to publicly display the work. "Display" is defined as showing a copy of a work, whether directly or by some indirect means. In the case of film, it includes nonsequentially showing the individual slides or frames.

The meaning of "publicly" is the same as above: where people gather, or where they may view the work even if they are not a friend or family member.

Everyday Application

When your favorite author draws a picture on a bookmark to go with your autographed copy of her book, you may want to hang it up in your home. But you shouldn't hang it in the public lobby of the office building at which you work.

Two More Limited Rights

In addition to the rights discussed above, two additional rights exist in certain cases and subject to specified limitations. These are the right of attribution and the right of integrity.

It's important to note that these rights are not part of the bundle of rights ordinarily considered as copyright. Rather, they are conferred only on creators of a limited-edition work of visual art.

In this context, "limited edition" means 200 or fewer copies of a single work, each of which has been numbered and signed by the creator. It does not include books or other works which can be mass produced. It also specifically excludes work for hire.

Attribution means that only the author can be credited with creating the work—not, for example, the printer or developer of the limited-edition copies. Furthermore, the author has the right to advertise herself as the creator of the work, even if she does not own the copyright (such as for a work made for hire, or if she has sold the copyright).

The right of *integrity* is meant to protect the author from a tarnishing of his reputation if another party, such as the printer or developer, mars, mangles, or otherwise blemishes the work, or if someone else copies the work. The right of integrity gives the author the right to say that he is not the author of the damage or of a copied work.

Note that U.S. copyright law applies to all creative works within the U.S., whether they originated in this country or not.

What Copyright Is Not

The Work

Copyright is *not* a book, song, or piece of art. Rather, copyright deals with how and, more importantly, by whom, a book, song, or other created work can be used. The work and the rights to the work are two separate and distinct things.

As they are different things, they may have different owners. The owner of a work might be, but also might not be, the copyright holder. You may own a book, but that does not mean you own the copyright to the book. In the same way, owning a photograph does not automatically mean you own the copyright to the photo.

Plagiarism

Copyright does not deal with plagiarism. Plagiarism is wrongfully claiming to be the author of a work. Breaching the terms of copyright does not constitute plagiarism, though both acts are a form of theft.

A person may copy a lovely poem, and claim that he wrote the poem. If that's not true, he has committed plagiarism. But unless he reproduces, adapts, distributes, or publicly performs or displays the poem, he has not infringed on the copyright.

On the other hand, a person may copy the lovely poem into her novel. If she gives credit to the poem's composer, she has not plagiarized the poem. But if she did not obtain permission from the copyright holder, she did infringe on the right to reproduce.

However, plagiarism and copyright infringement frequently occur together. People who dishonestly claim to have created a work often copy and distribute the work. In that case, both infractions have occurred.

Takeaway

The term *copyright* refers to the bundle of distinct rights that deal with how and by whom a work may be used.

They include the right to
- reproduce;
- adapt;
- distribute;
- publicly perform; or
- publicly display.

These rights are reserved exclusively for the owner of the copyright.

Chapter 2

Fair Use

One of the most misunderstood parts of copyright law may be the provision for fair use. The law states that "the fair use of a copyrighted work…for purposes such as criticism, comment, news reporting, teaching (including multiple copies for classroom use), scholarship, or research, is not an infringement of copyright."

This provision allows the limited use of copyrighted work without permission in certain cases. The law goes on to state four factors courts should consider in determining whether any particular use qualifies as fair:

> 1) the purpose and character of the use, including whether such use is of a commercial nature or is for nonprofit educational purposes;

2)   the nature of the copyrighted work;
3)   the amount and substantiality of the portion used in relation to the copyrighted work as a whole; and
4)   the effect of the use upon the potential market for or value of the copyrighted work.

Note that while these four factors *must* be considered, nothing prohibits other factors from also being considered.

Note also that the law does not state where to draw the line on any of the factors. It does not delineate which purposes or what natures may or may not qualify, or what amount or substantiality of either the original or the new work moves a use from fair to infringing, or how much effect a use may have on a copyrighted work. Nor does the law state which, if any, of these factors may have priority in consideration over the others. These are all legal gray areas.

With all these points left unspecified, how can an author ascertain whether his use qualifies as fair? Unfortunately, he'll only know for a certainty after he's sued and the court makes a ruling, since fair use is decided on a case-by-case basis.

But he can make an educated guess at some guidelines based on the way courts have interpreted this law in past cases.

- Educational uses are more likely to be considered fair than commercial uses.

- The more important the use is to the new work, the more likely it is to be considered fair.

- If the use is mostly comprised of facts, ideas, or other non-protected uses, the odds are in favor of being fair.

- Using the "heart" or "core" of a work is more likely to be considered infringing than using less essential parts.

- Borrowing a smaller part of a work is more likely to be approved than using a larger part.

- Likewise, when a smaller percentage of the new work is made up of the original work, the use is more likely to be fair than if a larger percentage was used.

- Rights are more strongly protected for more creative works. Similarly, more transformative uses are favored in fair use consideration.

- Audial and visual works (music and film) are more strongly protected than other types of work. Poetry also enjoys a high degree of protection.

- Extensive paraphrasing is likely to be considered infringing.

- If a use will cause the holder of the original

work to lose money, or her work to lose value, the use is unlikely to be considered fair. The law does not state that this factor must be given more weight than the other factors, but past cases show that it usually is.

• Using part of an unpublished work is less likely to be approved than using part of a published work.

• Satirical works are not likely to be considered fair, except for parody, which is.

Other Exceptions

The law provides for other limitations to the exclusive reservation of copyright laws. These include the right of libraries and archives to make one copy of a physical work they hold, and the right of hotels to rebroadcast certain transmissions. Both of these exemptions contain specified limitations.

Another exception is the right of any individual to sell a physical copy of a work they own. Selling your copy of this book for half the price you paid—or giving it away—in no way infringes on my copyright.

The final limitation has caused some confusion. This is the exemption of certain performances and displays for educational purposes. Many people take this section to mean that any use by a school, teacher, or student is exempt from copyright law, but that is not the case.

This section of the law does provide for the performance of display of a work by teachers and students (such as showing a film in class or the drama club performing a play). However, there are several criteria that must be met for this exemption to be lawful. For instance, the use must occur in a place devoted to instruction (like a classroom) and under the supervision of an instructor.

Additionally, the school must have in place policies regarding copyright which describe and promote compliance with copyright law, and these policies must be communicated to the staff and students.

These are only a few of the stipulations under which this exemption may be exercised. If you plan to use someone else's work in an educational setting, or to take advantage of any other exception to exclusive rights, be sure you understand and meet all the criteria. The aid of an intellectual property attorney will prove invaluable.

Takeaway

The provision for fair use and other exemptions to copyright allow limited use of protected works.

These uses are considered on an individual basis.

Courts will consider:
- the amount of original work used;
- the substantiality of the work used;
- how much of the new work is made up of the original;
- how creative or transformative the use is; and
- the purpose of the use.

Chapter 3

What Does Copyright Cover?

Copyright protects original, creative works of authorship fixed in a tangible medium of expression.

"Original" means the work was not copied.

"Creative" means it must come from the imagination or vision of the creator. Only a minimal amount of creativity is required; a mere "spark" of creativity fulfills this requirement. This is important, as it distinguishes a derivative work—one that is clearly based on a previous piece, as discussed under the right to adapt—from a transformative work that is inspired by another work, but is sufficiently different to merit being creative and thus does not infringe on the original artist's copyright.

"Tangible" means the work must be expressed in a

physical form that can be perceived, reproduced, or communicated. The work must exist in this physical form for more than a transitory duration to qualify as "fixed."

The following works of authorship are covered by copyright law:
- literary;
- musical, including lyrics;
- dramatic, including any accompanying music;
- pantomimes and choreographic;
- pictorial and graphic;
- sculptural;
- audiovisual, including motion pictures;
- sound recordings; and
- architectural works.

All eligible works are covered whether published or unpublished. The protection begins upon creation—the first time it is fixed in a physical medium. If the work is made over a period of time, any portion fixed at a particular time is considered created at that time. If in multiple versions are created, each version constitutes a separate work.

As of March 1, 1989, no notice or registration of any kind is required for copyright protections. It begins automatically upon creation. Before that date, notices were required.

However, the absence of a notice does not necessarily mean the work is free to use without permission. These works were given a chance to come into compliance and preserve the rights to the proper holder. Use the information in Chapter 6 to help determine whether a work that lacks notice is still protected.

What Copyright Does Not Cover

Since copyright covers very specific types of works, it follows that other types are not covered. The following do not fall under copyright protection:

- Titles or names, whether of a real or fictional person, place, book, painting, band, star, song, or any other thing;
- facts;
- ideas;
- concepts;
- systems;
- procedures;
- domains;
- short phrases;
- slogans;
- logos, unless the artwork contains sufficient authorship (a spark of creativity);
- intangibles, such as spoken words;
- work created by the U.S. government; or
- work in the public domain (for example, works published before 1924).

Let's look at a couple of examples, and then some special considerations. First we'll examine something frequently asked about: recipes.

Copyright law does not cover names or titles, including the name of recipes. Example:
GREAT-GRANNY'S REAL SOUTHERN CORNBREAD

Recipe ingredients are also not protected under copyright. They are considered a list, as below:

    1c flour
    ¾ c cornmeal
    1t salt
    1T baking power
    2 eggs
    1 c milk
    ¼ c melted butter
    1 T pure maple syrup

Following the list of ingredients in a recipe are the preparation instructions. Example:

Preheat oven to 375 degrees.
Sift dry ingredients together. Set aside.
Beat eggs.
Stir in milk, oil, and syrup.
Fold dry ingredients into wet ingredients.
Pour into well-greased 10" square pan.
Bake 30 minutes or until golden brown and an inserted knife comes out clean.

Procedures like the above also fall outside the realm of copyright. However, the *manner* of expression is protected. This may include the exact wording, how the directions are arranged on the page, and other such details.

Everyday Application

If someone wanted to let her neighbor know how to make this cornbread, or even use it in her own cookbook, she could do so as long as she expresses the directions in another way to keep from infringing on the method of expression above.

Example:

Mix wet and dry ingredients separately, then mix all together. Bake in a greased pan in a 375 degree oven for about 30 minutes.

The procedure is the same, but the manner of expressing that procedure differs.

Example 2

The piece of artwork in Example 2 includes a list of the states contained within a flag of the United States of America.

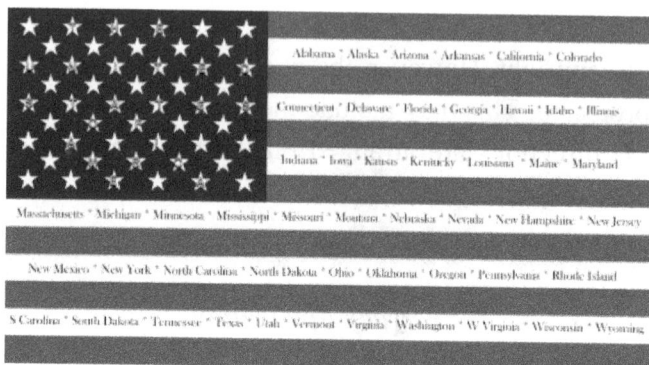

The list of states is not protected. And, an image of the US flag may be created by anyone. But putting them together in exactly this way, with the particular states per white line written in black Bookman Old Style, is protected by copyright.

Everyday Application

Suppose you wanted one of these. You know you can't copy this one, as that would infringe on the right to reproduce. But you know you can draw a flag, and you know you can list the states. So can you create your own version of this artwork?

Yes! The *idea* of listing states within a flag cannot be copyright protected—only this specific tangible expression of the idea is. If yours is not the same, you can create one.

Not the same? How different does it have to be? Unfortunately, the law does not define that. It's generally accepted that the new work must be different enough that an ordinary person would not confuse them. Using a different typeface in another color and adding a fringe around the edge would be ways to differentiate your creation from this one.

Considerations for Short Phrases

"Short" is not defined by copyright law, but one thing has been determined by case law: it has as much to do with creativity as it does with length. Before we get into that, let's examine why the law would refuse protection for phrases, and then a few "short" numbers.

One reason copyright law exists is to encourage creativity. Without protection, the lawmakers reasoned, it would be too easy for artists and authors to endlessly copy the same popular works, instead of channeling that energy into creating new works.

Likewise, if any and every short phrase were protected, eventually there would soon be no way to express anything at all, new or old. Imagine if the phrases "I am," "she looked," "it doesn't work," "how do you," and so forth could be used by only one person. Extrapolate that out, and eventually there would be no two words left to freely put together.

This is especially true with ideas. There are only so many ways to say, "They're in love" or "He wants revenge," or to draw a rose or a baby. Restricting the use of those few ways to one person would eliminate much of art and literature. Thus, neither ideas nor short phrases may be protected by copyright.

Now let's look at some numbers. Although there is no definition for "short," there are many opinions, both legal and surmised. Some of these include one or ten percent of a work, ten or twenty or three hundred words, or one line.

One of the most common interpretations is: about 10 words of a regular book. Using this interpretation, how much of a song could be used? Let's do the math. If an average book is 90,000 words, then ten words is about .0001%. And if an average song has 200 words in the lyrics, that percentage would equal .02 words, or less than one letter.

To be clear, there is no law stating that. It's simply an extension of one common understanding of "short" when dealing with copyright. But it demonstrates why writers and other artists are strongly cautioned against using any part of an essay, song, poem, or other work of relatively few words. A meaningful use may encompass a too-large percentage of the work to be exempted from copyright. See Chapter 2 for more information on this.

Remember, though, that creativity is as important as numbers when considering short phrases. There are cases in which phrases that would ordinarily be considered short have received copyright protection. This can happen when the phrase is particularly unique, or is the core of a work.

One court found that a single brief phrase could merit copyright if it "was so idiosyncratic in its treatment as to preclude coincidence." That is, a clever turn of phrase unlikely to be thought of by anyone else may indeed qualify for protection, even if it is few words.

If there's no definition of "short" in the law, how does an author know if the strung-together words she wants to quote are protected; or conversely, when she may prevent someone else from using her words? A court of law would have to make that determination on a case-by-case basis.

Considerations for Intangibles

An intangible thing is one without any physical presence, something that cannot be touched and held. Music, scents, and spoken words, for instance, are intangible. This does not mean, however, that any speech or music you hear may be used indiscriminately. There may be some tangible expression elsewhere; or, the intangible may be covered by some other form of protection.

Everyday Application

Suppose an author hears an interesting interview on the radio and uses some of the comments in her blog; or another writer overhears a great joke and puts it in his book.

He may later find that the person he heard tell the joke read it in a book; and she should know that radio programs, though spoken, are generally transcribed into written form.

In both cases, they've infringed on someone else's copyright.

Other Protection

It is important to realize that noncopyrightable items—lists, names, phrases, etc.—may fall under some other sort of protection. For example, patents protect discoveries and inventions. Words, phrases, logos, symbols, or designs may be covered by trademarks rather than copyright. (There is more information on trademarks in Chapter 11.)

Also, the specific expression of these items is copyrightable and may be protected.

Takeaway

Copyright protects original, creative works of authorship fixed in a tangible medium of expression.

Things not covered by copyright include titles, names, short phrases, and ideas, among other things.

However, the way these things are *expressed* can be copyright protected.

Chapter 4

Who Owns the Copyright?

The moment an original idea or vision is expressed in a fixed, tangible way, two types of property are born: the work itself as a physical property, and the rights inherent in the creation—the intellectual property.

Except in cases of work-for-hire, discussed below, both properties are owned by the creator until given away, sold, or otherwise conveyed. (The properties may be conveyed together or separately—see Chapter 10.) Nothing more has to happen; no registration or other action is required.

If there are multiple creators, as in a collaboration, each party has equal ownership in the copyright, regardless of the percentage of work each individual put into the creation. This applies to each person who contributed something independently copyrightable;

that is, who helped actually write the book or shape the sculpture. A person who provides only directions or ideas does not have a share of ownership in the rights, because directions and ideas are not copyrightable.

Work-for-Hire

A "work made for hire," or work-for-hire, is, as the name implies, a work created by someone who was hired to create it. This is often an employee or contractor of a company, such as the famed Imagineers who design theme parks for The Walt Disney Company or the employees of an advertising agency.

Only work created in the regular course of work as part of the artist's normal duties is considered work made for hire.

Everyday Application

If an employee of a newspaper writes an article for the newspaper, that would be a work-for-hire.

If the employee then goes home and writes a blog post on her website, that is not a work made for hire.

A work-for-hire may also be created by someone commissioned to provide one part of certain multi-party works, specifically:

- a contribution to a collective work (such as one essay or story in an multi-author anthology)
- a part of an audiovisual work
- a translation
- a supplementary work (such as an introduction, foreword, or illustrations in a book)
- a compilation
- an instructional text (such as a textbook)
- a test, or answer material for a test; or
- an atlas.

In these cases, there must be a written agreement signed by both parties which expressly states that the commissioned work will be considered a work made for hire. Work-for-hire belongs to the employer or commissioner, that is, the one paying for the creation.

Everyday Application

Suppose a staff reporter on the payroll and a freelance writer each submit an article to the local paper.

The newspaper owns the copyright to the reporter's article, but the freelance writer owns the rights to his.

Takeaway

The creator of a work owns its copyright.

Multiple creators share the rights equally.

An exception is work made for hire, in which case the copyright belongs to the one paying for the work to be done.

Chapter 6 deals with conveyance of copyright.

Chapter 5

How Long Does Copyright Last?

We've established that copyright begins at the moment of creation. When does it end?

That depends on several things:
- when the work was created;
- whether it was published, and if so when;
- whether notice was required and properly given; and
- whether renewal was required and properly performed.

The requirements for notice and for renewal have changed over the years. Whether any particular work is or was subject to either or both of these procedures is determined by which law was in effect on, or later became retroactively effective as of, the date the work was first published.

Unpublished Works

The copyright for unpublished works lasts for 70 years after the death of the author or creator. So the unpublished letters of James Dean, say, or an unpublished composition by Charlie Parker, both of whom died in 1955, will—unless the law changes before then—enter the public domain in 2025.

Everyday Application

Barring a change in law, if I were to die tomorrow (in the year 2019), rights to the unfinished drafts on my computer would expire in 2089.

Who would own the copyright in the meantime? See Chapter 10.

Public Domain

Works published before 1924 are in the public domain. Note: not *in* 1924, but through December 31, 1923.

This means "the public" owns these works, and they are available for anyone and everyone to use, in any way imaginable and without cost. Every use is already authorized by law, so no further permission is needed.

Attribution is still required; plagiarism is not permitted, even for works in the public domain.

Sometimes authors will find a photo or other work they want to use from the public domain, but are told that they must purchase a copy, or a license for the right to use it, from the holder of the actual work.

If you receive such a request, first ensure that the work is truly in the public domain. If there's doubt, ask the one claiming rights for proof of ownership to the copyright, not just to the work itself.

Frequently, you'll hear responses like, "It's my great grandmother," "I have the original," or "I already used that picture in my work." In such cases, the claimant has not learned the difference between the work itself and the rights to the work. (Or they've learned that most people will pay if asked.)

Works in the public domain do not require any permission from or fee to anyone for use. Not even to a museum, or a family member. No one. Period.

Furthermore, a mere copy or photograph of a work in the public domain is, itself, *also* in the public domain, because there hasn't been any significant transformation of the original work.

You are free to use these to your heart's content.

Other Works

The expiration of rights to works published in and after 1924 is not so easy to determine. Several criteria must be examined. The first of these is when the work was published.

Publication

In copyright law, "publication" is the distribution of copies of a work to the public by sale or other transfer of ownership, or by rental, lease, or lending.

Providing copies to a group for further distribution or public display constitutes publication.

Everyday Application

Theater staff designs a handbill for an upcoming performance, and delivers the specifications to be printed. The handbill is considered published when the printed copies are received by the company responsible for giving them out, even if printing took place earlier, and/or actual distribution to the public occurs later.

A public performance or display of a work does not of itself constitute publication.

> ### *Everyday Application*
>
> A publisher prints advance copies of a book that will be available for purchase several months later. Displaying an image of the book (as in advertisements), taking preorders, or even handing out a few free copies for review does not set the publication date. Making the book available to the general public for purchase does.

It's important to understand when publication occurs because that starts the countdown to the expiration of the rights to the work. But because copyright law has changed several times over the decades, there's not one duration that applies to all works.

Notice and Renewal

Whether copyright notice was required on a work and properly given is another factor that impacts when its copyright expires. From 1924 through February 28, 1989, notice of copyright was required on all published works. If the notice was given in the required manner, that's one criterion fulfilled; if not, the rights in that work were not reserved.

The next thing to check is whether renewal of the copyright notice was required. This applies to works published through 1963. If the renewal was not timely and properly performed, the rights were not reserved.

To complicate things even further, owners of works published between January 1, 1978 and February 28, 1989 had an opportunity to correct any omission of notice, and another change in the law automatically renewed the rights in works published from 1964 through 1977.

Generally, if all notices and renewals were supplied, the copyright endures 95 years for works published from 1924 through 1977.

Current Term

For works published after 1977, the copyright generally lasts for the lifetime of the creator plus an additional 70 years. If the work was made for hire or the author is unknown, the rights expire the earlier of 95 years from publication or 120 years from creation. This is the current law as of 2019. The copyright to the book you publish this year will have these terms (unless a future law changes it).

Note that U.S. copyright law applies to all creative works within the U.S., whether they originated in this country or not.

All Unpublished Works
Author's Life + 70 Years

Published before 1/1/2924

Public Domain

Published 1924—1963

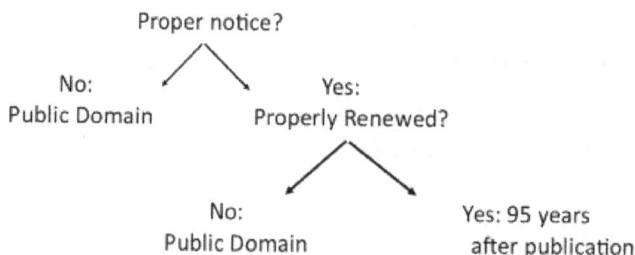

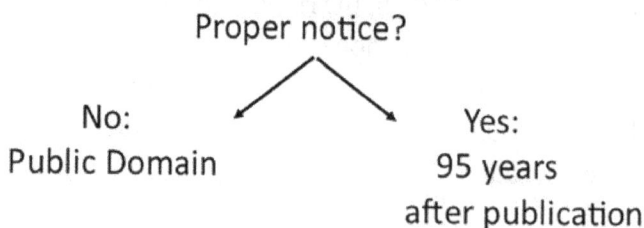

Proper notice?

No: Yes:
Public Domain   Properly Renewed?

No: Yes: 95 years
Public Domain   after publication

Published 1964—1977
Proper notice?

No: Yes:
Public Domain   95 years
                              after publication

NOTE: Rights to works created before 1978 but published between 1978 and 2002 will not expire before 2047, no matter when the author died.

Published 1978—Feb 1989

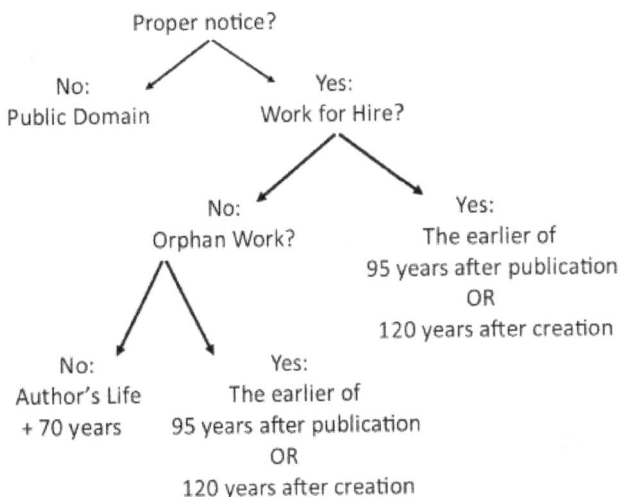

Proper notice?

No:
Public Domain

Yes:
Work for Hire?

No:
Orphan Work?

Yes:
The earlier of
95 years after publication
OR
120 years after creation

No:
Author's Life
+ 70 years

Yes:
The earlier of
95 years after publication
OR
120 years after creation

Published 3/1/1989 ➝

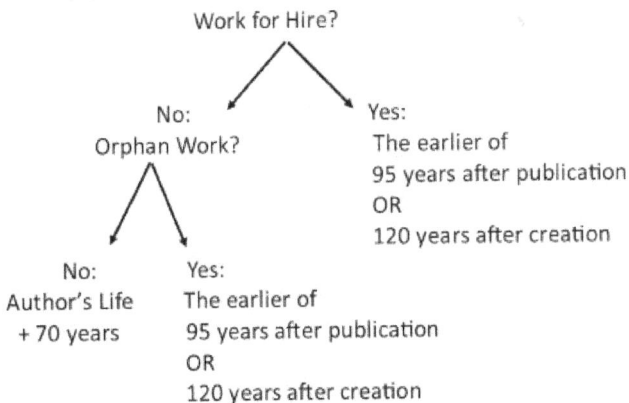

Work for Hire?

No:
Orphan Work?

Yes:
The earlier of
95 years after publication
OR
120 years after creation

No:
Author's Life
+ 70 years

Yes:
The earlier of
95 years after publication
OR
120 years after creation

Use the information on these pages to figure the copyright expiration on the next pages.

This work has the proper notice. Works published in 1964 are not subject to renewal, so we can ignore that fact. The copyright in books published from 1964 through 1977 expire 95 years after publication. Adding 95 to 1964 gives us 2059.

Note that copyright terms run through the end of the calendar year in which they expire, and enter the public domain on the first day of the following year.

The work above runs through 2059, so it will enter the public domain on January 1, 2060.

This one should be easy. Works published before 1924 are in the public domain.

If that's the case, why does does it include a statement that says no part of the book may be reproduced? Perhaps the publisher didn't know better; perhaps it's a bluff. More likely, it's simply a matter of standard policy to include the statement on any work the publisher puts out.

When a copyright notice contains more than one date, the earliest is the date that should be considered when calculating copyright requirements and term.

This book was first published in 1933, and the illustrations in 1953. So both are subject to notice and renewal. There is both a notice and a renewal for the illustrations, so the rights in them will expire 95 years after 1953, or 2048. They will enter the public domain on January 1, 2049.

There is a copyright notice for the text; but what about a renewal? An educated guess will let us assume that the second date, 1961, is a renewal date. If that's the case, both requirements are met and rights will expire 95 years after publication, or 2028, and enter the public domain on January 1, 2029.

To be certain, however, we would need to conduct a search with the US Copyright Office as described in Chapter 7. It so happens that this book, *Farmer Boy* by Laura Ingalls Wilder, had the copyright renewed on January 12, 1961 by her daughter Rose Wilder Lane, who inherited Wilder's literary estate. (See Chapter 10 for information on that.) Our educated guess is correct.

This is from the book *Ventures with Ideas*. What requirements should we look for?

Works published in 1952 are suject to both a notice and a renewal. We clearly see the notice. But how do we know if the copyright was renewed?

The renewal for any work published in 1951 or after was due in 1978 or after. Since all records from 1978 are in the online archives at copyright.gov we can search for these renewals.

Searches can be done by author's name, by title, and by the number. A search of all these criteria for this book will come up empty. This means there is no record of a renewal. If a work subject to renewal was not properly renewed, it entered the public domain, as this book did.

This one should be easy. Anything published before 1924 is in the public domain.

This one is a little tricky—so many dates! But we know to begin with the earliest—in this case, 1924. The book is subject to both notice and renewal. Again, the notice is obvious; but what about the renewal?

One would assume that at least one of the other dates is a renewal. A search of the online archives shows that the 1983 copyright was for a sound recording of the book. There is no record for *So Big* in 1982. Possibly a delay or error in paperwork caused some confusion as to the year of filing.

Records from before 1978 are not searchable at copyright.gov, but a search of the index at the Gutenburg Project shows that the copyright for *So Big* was renewed in 1951. This gives us all the information we need: since both requirements are met, this work is still protected.

When will it enter the public domain?

The copyright for works published in 1924 lasts for 95 years. That means the work is covered through 2019. On January 1, 2020, *So Big* will enter the public domain.

Takeaway

Several factors determine the duration of any particular copyright, including date of publication, whether notice was required and given, and whether renewal was required and performed.

Copyrights eventually expire, letting the work enter the public domain.

When a work enters the public domain, it is free for anyone to use however they wish, without cost and without permission or authorization of any kind from anyone.

Chapter 6

Protecting Your Rights

We've learned that copyright protection begins automatically the moment an original work is created in a tangible medium, and that there is no legal requirement for any kind of notice or registration to preserve those rights. Now let's look at why an author may wish to do so anyway.

One reason to supply a notice is as a courtesy. Placing a copyright notice is professional and polite, as doing so makes it easier for others to find out who owns the rights to works you create.

A more important reason may be that a copyright notice can help safeguard your rights by letting others know who to contact, either for permission to quote or otherwise use a part of the work, or if they see a use they suspect is unauthorized. If someone does use your work without permission, having the notice precludes them from claiming they didn't know it was copyrighted.

A proper notice of copyright consists of three elements:

- the word "copyright," the abbreviation "copr," or the © symbol (the letter C in a circle);
- the owner's name; and
- the year of publication.

Examples:

- © Teresa Lynn 2019;
- Copyright 2019 Teresa Lynn

Nothing more is needed, though one may wish to add, where space allows, information on how to contact the holder.

Registration

Registration of a work is different from providing notice of copyright. Unlike providing notice, registration is required. This entails providing some information about the work and the person who holds the rights to it, along with a specified number of copies of the work (generally two), to the U.S. Copyright Office. Copyright law requires this to be done within three months of publication.

But haven't we established that nothing need be done to create copyright, that it's automatic upon creation?

Yes, we have. The registration requirement is not a condition of copyright protection; that exists whether the owner complies with the registration requirement or not.

Nonetheless, the Copyright Office is entitled by law to collect copies of every work published in the United States, to ensure that the Library of Congress* will have access to it if desired. If these copies are not sent voluntarily, the Registrar may demand them, and enforce fines of up to $2750 plus the price of the copies on owners who do not comply.

In addition, in the case of unauthorized use of a work, no suit for copyright infringement may be brought until registration of the work is completed. In other words, you can't sue someone for stealing your work unless you've registered it.

Note that "poor man's copyright" is not a substitute for registration. This is the belief that mailing a copy of the work to oneself, and then not opening the package when it's received, proves the work had been created by the sender as of the date of the postmark. There is no provision for this system in the law, and therefore it is not sufficient either to bring suit for infringement or to comply with registration.

*I mentioned the Library of Congress. If the author sends the work to the Library of Congress, this does not satisfy the required copyright registration. To comply with copyright law, copies of the work must be sent to the Registrar of Copyrights.

What if Your Work Is Stolen?

It's becoming more and more common for authors to find their work used without authorization. This may include anything from copying and reposting an image or part of a blog post to republishing an entire book—with or without claiming authorship—and selling it to someone else. If this happens, there are measures you can take to terminate the unlawful use.

First, document the offense. Note when, how, where, and by whom the use occurred—or at least as much as is known. Include how the matter came to your attention, and any other persons you know of who witnessed it. Record the full domain name of online occurrences. If possible, take photos or screenshots of the use.

An infringed-upon author may wish to immediately file suit. This is certainly one option (provided she has properly registered the work); but she may wish to consider other alternatives first. Depending on the manner of use, there are a few things she can do to try to resolve the situation.

- Ask the user to remove the unauthorized copy from print and/or the web. This is the simplest, most direct approach. Usually, once discovered, the user will stop rather than risk legal action.

- If you have a publisher, notify them and let them handle it. Your publishing contract most likely provides for this.

- If the wrongful use is in a published work, notify that publisher. No legitimate publisher wants to print plagiarized or unlawful works.

- If the unauthorized use is online, send a DMCA (Digital Millennium Copyright Act) notice to the internet service provider. You can find templates for such notices online.

- If the unauthorized work is being sold by a third party, notify the seller that the copy is unauthorized.

If these recourses fail, it's probably time to consult an intellectual property attorney.

An infringed-upon author should not engage in libel or slander against the other party. It may be easy to speak ill of one who has wronged us, but an author who doesn't guard his words may find himself on the other side of the litigation table. He may also find his own reputation tarnished from the backlash.

Takeaway

Providing notice of copyright is not required, but it is professional.

Registration of new literary works is required.

If you work is used without authorization, try to resolve the situation as soon as possible, and engage an attorney if necessary.

Chapter 7

How to Find a Copyright Owner

If you need to find the rights holder of any particular work, the first place to look is on the work itself. Most published works contain a copyright notice, as discussed in the previous chapter.

Many times, the work also contains information on how to contact the holder. For example, on the copyright page of this book, you will see beneath the copyright notice a short explanation for those unfamiliar with copyright, followed by the contact information of the publisher. If a person wanted to use a part of this book for some reason, they should contact the publisher.

If there is no contact information, look for clues that may lead you to the person or company you seek. In the case of a book, in addition to the author's name and the publisher, look in the acknowledgements for the name of an editor or literary agent. Even if these persons (or agencies) don't own the copyright, they may be able to provide information as to whom you should contact.

Everyday Application

One book may provide multiple sources to check for a copyright owner. First look at all the names on the copyright page. Then look at any additional names on the title page. We can also check the acknowledge-ments. In this book,we can find at least eight names to track down and inquire for the copyright owner.

Text © 1979 Charles K. Kliment and Hilary Louis Doyle
© Argus Books Ltd. 1979

Typeset by Inforum Ltd., Portsmouth
Printed in Great Britain by A. Wheaton & Co., Ltd., Exeter

BELLONA PUBLICATIONS
ARGUS BOOKS LTD,
ARGUS HOUSE,
14 ST JAMES RD.,
WATFORD,
HERTS.

Acknowledgements

The authors and publishers wish to thank the following for assistance in the production of this book: Mr Tom Jentz for his invaluable help in research;

Sometimes, there may be no copyright notice or information of any kind. Perhaps it was removed, either purposely or by accident, at some point since production. Or maybe the work never contained the information to begin with.

In these situations, you may find what you need at the US Copyright Office. If the work was published in 1978 or after and was properly registered, it should be listed in the online search of registered works (see Resources at the end of this book). You can search by name of the author, title of the work, or keyword, in addition to document or registration number.

Everyday Application

Copyright.gov

Results for your search will display in a list. Click on the item you wish to see, and the copyright claimant's name and contact information will be shown, along with the name and contact information for rights and permissions.

Why would the contact for permission be different from that of the claimant? This happens when any of the rights have been sold or assigned—as when one or more of the rights is purchased from an author by a publisher. More information on this can be found in Chapter 10.

If the work was published before 1978, a manual search will have to be done. If you live near the Washington, D.C. area, you can make arrangements to do this yourself; otherwise, you'll need to have the Office search for you. See Resources at the end of this book for more information.

Orphan Works

Some works were never registered. And sometimes the registered information is outdated and no longer relevant. This can happen when a company that held rights was bought out, merged with another company, or simply closed up. In other cases, the original copyright holder may have passed away.

Works which have no verifiable copyright owner are known as orphan works. Many people believe orphan works are fair game, usable in the same was as those in the public domain, but the law does not make that provision. If the work was published after 1924 and was registered and renewed in accordance with laws in effect at the time, then the rights are still reserved to someone, whether the someone is known or not.

If the work is orphaned due to closure of a business or death of a holder, you can try to determine who may have purchased, inherited, or otherwise obtained the rights using the information in Chapter 10.

Obtaining Permission for Use

Once you've determined who holds the rights to a work, you can ask for permission to quote or otherwise use the work.

A rights holder will usually want to know certain things before granting this permission, such as:

- Information about you (or the author requesting permission):
  - Your name
  - Your previous published works
  - Your contact information

- Information about the copyrighted work you wish to use:
  - Its title
  - Its author or creator
  - Its publisher
  - Any identifier, such as the ISBN of a book
  - Exactly what part of the work you wish to use, such as the number of lines or words
  - The type of permission you're seeking— usually the non-exclusive right to reproduce and distribute

- Information about the proposed use:
  - The purpose of the use—commercial, in the case of a book you plan to sell. Other uses may be educational, commentary, research, etc.
  - The medium and genre
  - Title of the work
  - Name and contact information of publisher, along with date of publication. You may provide an anticipated or estimated publication date if one has not yet been set.
  - (Anticipated) number of copies—remember that if you get permission for a specified number of copies, you'll need additional permission for more copies
  - (Anticipated) sales price
  - The countries and/or language(s) in which the work will be distributed—often stated as "worldwide in all languages."

Including all the above information in the original request can eliminate the need for back-and-forth communications, thus saving time. A well-written, professional letter stating that you are seeking permission for use of copyrighted material, followed by all necessary information as outlined above, will suffice.

As a general rule, the easier you make it for the owner to grant permission, the more likely you are to receive a favorable response. That's why letters of request often conclude with something like the following:

> If the terms described herein are satisfactory, please specify how to credit the material in the space below, sign, and date. If there are fees or other conditions, please include such information. Your signature shall grant permission for the above-requested use, as well as affirm your right to do so. You may return this letter in the enclosed self-addressed, stamped envelope.

You may also wish to ask them to provide any information they may have concerning the copyright holder, in the event that you've reached the wrong party.

Lastly, be sure to thank them for their consideration of your request; and if they do grant permission, send a separate note of appreciation.

Takeaway

There are several places to search for a copyright holder. These include on the work itself and at copyright.gov.

A polite, professional letter that includes all information about the work and your proposed use often results in permission.

Chapter 8

Online Works: How Are They Different?

Say you need an image for your website, and you find the perfect one online. What's more, you can see that the image has been used on several other websites, and none of them give credit to anyone. Since it's all over the internet already, and since it has no credit, anyone is free to use it, right?

That's one of the biggest myths about copyright. And that's just what it is: a myth. The truth is that online works are subject to the same copyright laws as every other creative work. There is no difference.

Many people believe that as long as they link the used image or other work back to the site from which they obtained it, they are giving proper attribution and that this makes the use legal. There are two areas in which this is incorrect.

First, a link-back is not an attribution. Attribution includes providing the name of the original creator, as well as additional information.

More to the point of copyright law, attribution or giving credit for a work is not permission. Nor is it an exemption under the fair use provision. It is simply not legal to use other peoples' work without permission, regardless of whether the new work or the original one, or both, are online. Once you have permission, you give attribution when you use it.

Another myth is that stating "No copyright infringement intended" is an acceptable defense. This isn't true either.

Everyday Application

Online works have exactly the same protections and fall under the same laws regarding use as other works. Always obtain permission.

Think about what would happen if a stranger (or even a friend) took your car without asking. You notify the police and eventually the vehicle is spotted speeding down the highway in another town. Now imagine that the person driving it says, "But officer,

I didn't *intend* to steal it. It just makes my work so much easier." You probably wouldn't consider that an acceptable excuse.

That seems like a silly example, but it's apt. Unless it's a legally fair use, the unauthorized copying or using of another's work in any way, including online, is an act of theft, whether the user "intends" it to be or not.

If unsure whether the use would qualify as fair, the safe course is to obtain written permission before using any work to which you don't own the copyright.

Creative Commons

Another myth regarding the use of online works is that any work found in the Creative Commons is free to use. This is only partly right.

Creative Commons is a non-profit organization that provides special copyright licenses. These licenses allow creators to give the public access to their work(s) under terms set by the creator. While it is true that one of these licenses allows free use for any purpose without permission, not all of them do.

It is therefore very important to take note of the type of license of any work you wish to use from Creative Commons. A CC Zero, or CC0, license, indicates that the owner has kept zero rights reserved, and allows any and all use. In addition to (or possibly instead of) the type of license, there may be a phrase such as "No (copy)right(s) reserved" or "Dedicated to the public domain," or the copyright symbol with a slash through it.

Any work not designated as above still retains some of it inherent rights. Search the Creative Commons website to learn which rights are retained and which are given up for any particular license.

Takeaway

Online works have exactly the same protections and fall under the same laws regarding use as other works. Always obtain permission.

(Yes, that's a repeat of the Everyday Application. It bears repeating.)

But there are places to find works to use, such as Creative Commons.

Chapter 9

Special Considerations

Book Covers and Illustrations

The cover of a book, as well as any illustrations, graphs, etc. found within it, usually have separate rights from the book itself. There are cases in which these items were either produced by the book's author or created as works for hire; but usually, these have their own creator who owns the rights to them.

This is true even if you pay someone to draw or otherwise produce the works for you. Remember, to qualify as a work-for-hire, there must be a written agreement stating that specifically.

Lacking such agreement, payment to the artist is not purchasing the rights to the artwork, but merely a copy of it, and, likely, a license to use it in your book.

The contract you have with the artist will determine whether this is a one-time right, or if you may use the same cover on different versions (such as for a paperback and an e-book). It pays to read the fine print carefully and be sure the payment covers all uses you wish to procure.

If an artist uses any material from another party to create the artwork, such as from a stock photo company, a license will need to be secured from that party as well. This is something else the contract should specify: will you or the artist be responsible for obtaining a license to use elements such as stock photos or models? The minimum rights required should be outlined. You don't want to end up with a stock photo that can only be used one time when you plan to use it in a series.

Does this mean you cannot use the cover art in advertisements? This seems to be another gray area.

A "useful article" is defined as one which has an intrinsic utilitarian function other than merely to portray the appearance of the article or to convey information. Any element of such an item is likewise a useful article in its own right.

The useful article provision of copyright law states:
In the case of a work lawfully reproduced in useful articles that have been offered

for sale or other distribution to the public, copyright does not include any right to prevent the making, distribution, or display of pictures or photographs of such articles in connection with advertisements or commentaries related to the distribution or display of such articles, or in connection with news reports.

Some attorneys say book covers qualify as useful articles since they are used in the promotion or advertising of a book, or in reviewing, commentary, or other such uses that go beyond mere appearance or information.

I don't know of any cases where this has been argued in a court. The safest course would be to make sure any agreement for cover art or other artwork contains explicit permission to use the artwork in advertising, as well as any other use you may wish to make of it.

Everyday Application

Graphics, including book covers and interior images of any kind, have rights separate from the book's.

A contract should clearly outline all uses permitted of the graphics.

Music

Copyright for music can be doubly complicated. This is because, generally, music is doubly protected.

The composition holds one copyright. Composition includes the lyrics and the specific arrangement of musical notes. If these were created by different persons, the copyright would vest in the parties jointly and equally. Often, these rights are assigned to a music publisher, but that is not always the case. What's more, the lyricist(s) and arranger(s) may have different publishers.

An author who wishes to use lyrics in a book should carefully review the factors regarding Fair Use, as well as the consideration of short phrases.

- Any meaningful quotation would probably encompass a substantial portion of the song.
- If she plans to sell her book, this commercial use will be for her profit—something courts typically consider to a greater degree than other factors.
- Music is generally accorded stronger protection than some other types of works.

In light of the above, it would be imprudent to use song lyrics and claim the use is fair. If an author is intent on using part of a song, he should contact the publisher and inquire about obtaining a license.

Or, he can consider using the title of the song instead of its lyrics. As you will recall, titles do not fall under copyright protection. However, the author should take care not to use the title in promotion, or he may inadvertently violate trademark protection.

Another option might be to find a similar song in the public domain.

An artist's recording of a song holds a separate copyright. Usually, the recording company holds these rights. When any additional musicians cover the song, their recordings are likewise copyrighted.

Until recently, a book author had no need to be concerned with this second set of rights, because there was no way to include an audial recording in a book. With the advent of audiobooks, that is no longer the case. If an author has permission to use lyrics in her work, she should ensure that this license includes any recording she uses in her audiobook.

Everyday Application

Use of lyrics is discouraged, as too many factors weigh against it being fair.

Titles, or songs in the public domain, may be used.

Film & Video

Where music typically has two copyrights, film and video may have many more. This could impact an author who creates book trailers or other video uses.

Films and videos, whether movies, television shows, or other forms, generally require a number of creators, each of whom may hold their own copyright. Some of these may include actors, narrators or voice-over artists, the composer(s) and performer(s) of the soundtrack, the cameraman, and others. Some (or even all) of these may have been working for hire, but this can never be assumed.

In addition, use of film often requires permission from and payment to various guilds, such as the Screen Actors Guild-American Federation of Television and Radio Artists, the Writers Guild of America, and the Directors Guild of America, among others.

Even if a film has entered the public domain, rights to some elements of it, such as the soundtrack, may still be protected. The various rights in film can be so complicated that any use should be done under advisement from an intellectual property attorney.

Takeaway

Book covers and graphics, music, and film or video may all have multiple copyright holders.

Permission must be obtained from each and every owner.

Use of music and video will likely not be considered fair.

An intellectual property attorney should be consulted.

Chapter 10

Conveyance

We've learned that certain rights, considered together as copyright, are automatically vested in the author of a work upon its creation. Now let's consider the ways and means in which these rights may be conveyed to others, and why.

One way copyright may convey is by involuntary transfer. This is when a court orders a transfer due to bankruptcy, divorce, or other such circumstances. Fortunately, this type of assignment is relatively rare.

Some of the most common grants of copyright occur when a publisher purchases rights to an author's literary work, or when one musician "covers" another's songs.

There is also a transfer that often happens without

either party—the one conveying or the one receiving the rights—knowing it: inheritance.

A transfer, also called an assignment, of rights is a complete conveyance of all rights forever. It must be executed in writing, signed by the grantor.

A license, also known as permission, may be conveyed orally or in writing. It may be:

Exclusive	*Non-exclusive*
Only the named licensee can use the rights granted; even the owner can't use those rights	*The owner may allow others to use the work, and may continue to use the work herself*
For a specified time	*For a specified time*
Unlimited	*May have limitations (area, language, etc.)*

When a publisher purchases rights to a book, it is generally an exclusive license for the right to reproduce and distribute (also called "publish"). No one else may exploit these rights for as long as the publisher holds the license.

The publishing contract will outline any limitations to the rights the publisher is receiving. It is very important to read the contract carefully and ensure that it grants only the rights you wish to convey and specifies any limitations desired.

Note that reputable publishers do not require an assignment or transfer of the copyright (known as a "copyright grab"). Rather, they obtain a license— permission—to exploit certain rights subject to certain limitations. The author retains ownership of the copyright. Reputable publishers register the copyright in the author's (and illustrator's, if applicable) name.

Self-published authors do not need to grant rights to anyone, but may choose to provide a license to, for example, an audiobook recording company or a film studio.

Everyday Application

Authors tend to get excited when a book is accepted for publication. Don't let that stop you from carefully reading the contract and understanding every clause.

It's typical for publishers to require an exclusive license; but they should never require you to transfer your rights.

Literary Estates

If you're a writer, you have literary assets known collectively as a literary estate. Your literary estate is comprised of all your writings, both published and unpublished, as well as all your rights to those writings whether subject to any license or not, and any licenses you may hold.

As with any other type of asset, property, or estate, provision should be made for a literary estate's management in case of the author's incapacity or death—because, just as in the other cases, someone will inherit this estate.

Section 201 of the copyright law states that "ownership of a copyright may be...bequeathed by will or pass as personal property by the applicable laws of intestate succession."

If you care what happens to the unpublished drafts in your drawer, or the royalties from your publisher, take steps to ensure that your wishes concerning these things are clear. Otherwise, your literary assets may be treated as Hemingways' were: In his lifetime, he verbally told people he wanted his unpublished works destroyed after his death, but did not mention them in his will. When he died, all his works, both early and unfinished, were published—and not to great acclaim.

Following are some things to consider.

Your Unpublished Works

You may wish to list them, and next to each one designate whether you wish the work itself to be

- destroyed;
- given to a particular person; or
- published.
  - Who do you wish to complete or edit the work and pursue publication?
  - Is self-publication acceptable?
  - If not, and no publisher accepts it, what is Plan B?

You will also need to designate the recipient of the rights to each of these works. Of course, for works you wish to be published, the rights should be bequeathed to the individual you wish to complete the work (if necessary) and pursue publication.

But when the physical copy of a work is left to a particular person, you may or may not wish that individual to also receive the rights to it. Be clear about your wishes for both the work itself and, separately, the rights to it.

Including where each unpublished work can be found will be helpful, especially in the case of old manuscripts hidden in the back of a closet.

Your Published Works

You may wish to list these, along with the publisher and royalty, and next to each one designate who should receive any royalties. Someone will need to notify the publishers of this change in royalty recipient upon your death.

Since any publisher has (or at least should have) only limited rights and does not own the copyright, you need to bequeath ownership of the copyright. This will include any rights that revert from the publisher, such as at the end of the publishing contract term.

Your Licenses

Where you have received permission to use quotations, artwork, lyrics, or other such licensed uses, you may wish to list each one along with its expiration date.

For published works and licenses, include where to find a copy of the contract or other documentation.

A Literary Executor

A writer may wish to appoint a literary executor in their will. A literary executor is different from the general executor of the estate. This person is concerned only with your literary assets.

The powers of the literary executor last as long as any copyrights and licenses do, so she will likely be handling the literary estate for decades.

Immediate duties of the literary executor include ensuring that all the proper entities are notified of changes and any required paperwork is properly and timely completed. She would also destroy any copies so designated, and work with publishing companies and other agencies to transfer royalties and rights as required.

In the long term, she would be responsible to:

- capitalize on any unpublished works you wish to be pursued;

- make decisions on any works not provided for;

- make decisions regarding license requests, renewals, and terminations;

- maintain copyrights; and

- bring suit against infringers.

This is not an exhaustive list, but is provided to show the extent of the literary executor's duties.

One thing she would not be able to do is terminate certain agreements. By law, only the author's heirs may do this. However, the literary executor may advise the heirs.

There are other issues to consider in appointing a literary executor. Some of these include:

- Will she receive compensation? If so, how will it be calculated, and will there be provisions for changes to such in the future?

- How will she pay expenses on behalf of the literary estate?

- What provisions will be made if she becomes unable to fulfill her duties?

As you can see, there are many considerations. An intellectual property attorney can help you navigate this unfamiliar and complicated process.

Everyday Application

If you haven't planned for your literary estate, now is a good time to start. An intellectual property attorney should be consulted.

Takeaway

Copyright may be given away, sold, or bequeathed just as any other property can.

Make sure you read contracts and license agreements carefully to ensure conveyences are in accordance with the terms you desire.

Provide for your literary estate.

Chapter 11

Trademarks

If titles, names, phrases, and logos aren't copyrightable, can an author title her book *To Kill a Mockingbird* and use a mockingjay pin on the cover? Can she name her character Harry Potter or Meryl Streep? And can that character eat at Taco Bell and ask, "Got milk?"

These questions are answered in trademark law. A trademark, like a copyright, is a form of protection for intellectual property. Several items in the "not copyrightable" list of Chapter 2, including names, titles, slogans, short phrases, and symbols or designs, can fall under trademark protection.

Trademarked property may be marked with either of two symbols. The ® symbol stands for "registered." It signifies that the word or image to which it's affixed is registered with the US Patent & Trademark Office (USPTO). The other trademark symbol is ™. This symbol is for trademarks that have been established by use as representing a company or product, but have not been registered. It gives notice that the mark's owner will defend it against infringement.

Trademarks must be renewed every 10 years, plus an initial renewal after 5 years, but may renewed into perpetuity. They don't expire as long as they are used in connection with goods or providers in commerce.

Anything used to identify a company or a product and differentiate it from similar companies or products may be trademarked. Words or images are most often used to represent a product or its source, but characters, sounds, and even scents can also be trademarked. The expression must be recognizable— that is, distinct enough that it will not be confused with another similar word, image, or so forth.

The McDonald's M is an example of a protected design. Other companies might develop a logo or symbol that uses an M in some way, but it wouldn't look like the golden arches. No matter where you are in the world, that yellow M means a Big Mac and Chicken McNuggets. Those products are also trademarked, by the way. Other eateries may have chicken bites, tenders, strips, or even nuggets, but only McDonald's has Chicken McNuggets. The slogan *I'm lovin' it* and the 5 musical notes that precede it each have a trademark, as well.

Let's examine some ways trademarks may affect writers.

Titles

Generally, a title is not eligible for trademark protection, because a title doesn't identify the source (such as the author or publisher) of the product. It's merely descriptive of the book itself. However, when a title becomes so well known that it becomes a brand in itself, it may become trademarked. *Little House on the Prairie* falls into this category.

Book series are much more likely to become trademark eligible than single book titles. When a series becomes known, its title differentiates that particular set of book from all the other sets of books in the marketplace. At the same time, the series title identifies all the books in the set as coming from the same author. Some examples are Harry Potter, Nancy Drew, and Game of Thrones.

Names/Characters

As with titles, if a character reaches a level of fame where its name and/or likeness are recognized and associated with a source—whether an author or publisher—it may be trademark protected. Mickey Mouse, for instance, is practically synonymous with Disney. Black Panther and Spider-Man are known to be Marvel characters.

Using a Trademarked Brand in a Book

Typically, mention of a trademarked brand is permissible as a fair use. Under trademark law, there are two kinds of fair use. *Descriptive use* allows a writer to use a trademark to describe the products; *nominative use* allows reference to actual goods associated with the trademark. As with copyright, trademark fair use of either type is something to be decided by a court of law on a case-by-case basis.

In general, though, the action of a book can take place in Six Flags and the antagonist can eat Frosted Flakes with no problem. However, the author must not dilute the brand. That is, the book should not confuse the reader as to the source of the product. If the character eating Frosted Flakes said it was a great Post cereal (it's actually a Kellogg's product), the author might face consequences for trademark infringement.

Some brands become generic from years of use. At one time, aspirin and kerosene were trademarked brands. Now, they are generic words for any acetylsalicylic acid painkiller and distilled petroleum. A problem occurs when a still-trademarked word is used generically. Thus, a character should not "google information" about the town he's moving to; rather, he should "search Google for information."

Writers should also avoid implying the brand has an affiliation with the book. That means the cover image should not show the Six Flags logo (unless the author receives permission, of course). Using the park's name in the title or description would not be wise, either. These things make it seem as if Six Flags has endorsed the book.

Nor should the book portray any brand in a negative light. If the story set in Six Flags is a murder mystery, the murderer should probably not turn out to be an employee there, and the method by which the victim is killed should not involve a unique aspect of the park. Doing this may tarnish the brand by injuring its commercial value. Instead, create a fictional park, and make it different enough from Six Flags that a reader wouldn't recognize it as that particular brand of theme park.

Merchandise

When a character or title achieves trademarked status, any related merchandise generally enjoys the same trademark protection. An author may refer to these in the same manner she would any other brand: Mia pulled on her favorite Star Wars shirt.

Fan Fiction

Fan fiction is fiction based on the character, plot, or setting of another work. As the name implies, these spin-offs are written by fans of the existing book, usually as an expression of how much they enjoy the original. The new stories may place beloved characters in different situations or relationships, or introduce fresh characters to an intriguing story world.

It is commonly believed that fan fiction is a fair use. This is not the case. Almost by definition, fan fiction is an adapted or derivative work. As we learned in Chapter 1, the right to adapt is part of copyright, and is reserved to the original creator. Thus, most fan fiction is copyright infringement. If the characters have reached trademark status, fan fiction infringes on that as well.

Not only is the existing story protected by copyright, but its fictional characters may enjoy their own separate copyright protection, in addition to their trademark protection. Copyright law protects characters that are sufficiently unique and distinctive, as opposed to "stock characters."

A ninja, for example, is a stock character. A ninja who is a teenaged turtle is unique. An orphan is a stock character, but an abandoned young girl who raises herself in the marsh is unique. While a dog is a stock character, a dog who loves car racing and believes he'll be reincarnated as a human merits his own copyright protection.

Still, fan fiction flourishes because some authors choose to allow it, or even encourage it. They appreciate that fans have such connection with their characters, and they may consider the new stories as a type of free advertising. But other authors have different views. Some are indifferent, and some are opposed to anyone else's use of their work.

An author whose work inspires fan fiction should inform his fans in a kind but firm way of his limitations on the use of his work—for example, J.K. Rowling permits fan fiction about Harry Potter, but with the caveats that it not be pornographic, and that it remain a non-commercial activity.

The author should also consult an intellectual property attorney regarding his legal options under both copyright and trademark law. He will then be in a position to make an informed decision about how to respond to his fans' appropriation of his work.

If an author wishes to write fan fiction, she should

remain within the limits set by the original author. If she's absolutely determined to do more than that, she should use the original work as no more than an inspiration, and should remove, change, or delete enough elements that her use is transformative, instead of merely derivative. She might also include a disclaimer that she is not the creator of, and does not own rights to, the original work, and give credit to the one who does.

A fan fiction writer using a character in the public domain as a basis should be sure he does not inadvertently use copyrighted material. If his story based on *The Legend of Sleepy Hollow* casts Ichabod Crane as a constable, he's likely encroaching on the protected Johnny Depp portrayal, instead of sticking to the original story featuring a schoolmaster.

Takeaway

Trademark is distinct from copyright and covers some intellectual property that copyright does not.

There may be some overlap, where characters fall under the protection of both copyright and trademark.

Mentioning trademarked brands is generally acceptable if the use does not dilute or tarnish the brand.

Fan fiction is an infringement but is often tolerated.

Chapter 12

Other Limitations

Can a writer use a real person or business in her work? Does it make any difference if the person she wishes to write about is famous, or whether they are alive or dead? Does it matter how much of the work concerns the real person, or whether what she writes is true or made up for the sake of the story?

These questions fall outside the realm of copyright law; but since they often come up when discussing rights, let's examine the use of real persons and organizations.

In general, such use is allowed. It does not matter whether the person is famous or unknown, or dead or alive. However, there are at least three considerations to keep in mind when doing so. These are libel, privacy, and publicity.

Libel

Libel is the publication of a defamation of character. It's the written or other physical communication of a false statement that harms a person's reputation, made to anyone other than the defamed person.

Libel is:

- Untrue
- Factual
- Believable
- About a living person(s) or an existing organization
- Identifiable
- Made with malice

To qualify as libel, a statement must be untrue. An author can write about someone's most detestable acts, and as long as what she says is true, the statements are not libelous. She should, however, be prepared to prove them true if challenged.

Only factual statements can be libelous. How can an untrue statement be factual? In this case, factual means that the statements are not merely expressing an opinion, but are expressed as facts. This is because the first amendment protects everyone's right to publish their opinions.

> ### *Everyday Application*
>
> If I say my neighbor is a misogynist, I'm stating a subjective opinion that can be neither proved nor disproved. But if I say he published a letter to the editor in yesterday's local paper stating all the reasons he thought women should not be given promotions, I'm making a factual statement which can be proven as either true or false.

One court held that a statement is libelous only if it can be "reasonably understood as stating actual fact." The court said assertions must be examined in context, and implied that even statements which some intelligent people might believe are not libelous if, when read as a whole, the statement is too improbable for that belief to be reasonable.

> ### *Everyday Application*
>
> Stating my neighbor wrote a such letter might be taken as true by many people; but if I claim he met with aliens to draft a letter that could brainwash readers into believing it, it should be clear to most people that the statement is too absurd to be taken seriously.

One court has held that the *expectation* of belief matters. If a writer makes a false statement, whether knowingly or not, that she expects her readers to believe, she may be liable whether or not the readers do, in fact, believe it.

Only a living person or group of people or an existing company would care about their reputation. Thus, any assertion about a dead person or defunct organization cannot, by definition, be libelous. It may be possible, though, to inadvertently defame living persons when the intention is to speak only of the dead. For example, stating that a deceased CEO led a company full of fraudsters implies that everyone in the company—including all the current, living employees—commits fraud.

Not only must the person be living, they must be identifiable. An author who wishes to base his character on a real individual may do so, but if he writes anything defamatory, he would do well to ensure that his character is different enough that readers won't realize its inspiration. Even if the writer changes the name and some characteristics of the real person, if enough characteristics or traits are similar to the real person that readers recognize her, untrue derogatory remarks may be considered libelous. This most often happens in memoirs and auto/biographies, but may also occur in fiction.

A final consideration for libel is "actual malice." This does not necessarily mean that the author intended to be malicious or defame the person. Simply knowing that a disparaging remark is untrue may be considered actual malice, as may reckless disregard or negligence. So even if a writer did not know the statement he made was untrue, if he should have known, or could have known if he'd checked his sources and facts, he may still be liable.

Actual malice may come into play well after a libelous statement is made. Consider this scenario: a writer posts defamatory remarks she does not know to be false on her blog. Someone who does know the comments are untrue informs the writer of the facts, but the writer is busy and doesn't make time to correct the post. Eventually she forgets about it. A year later, the defamed person sees the post. He may bring suit against her for each day the post was published after the writer learned her remarks were false.

Everyday Application

When writing about, or mentioning, a real person or organization, check your facts, and re-check them. Then check them again. And if you ever learn different, make corrections.

Privacy

Another consideration when writing about a real person is the expectation of privacy.

Everyone has facets of their life they do not wish to be known by the general public. Even celebrities keep some things to themselves or those close to them. And we all have the right to do so. Invasion of this right by the public disclosure of private facts is unlawful.

Invasion of privacy consists of:

- Disclosing private facts that are not of public interest;

- Intruding into a person's secluded life; or

- Presenting someone in a false light or in an offensive manner.

As with libel, privacy infringement must in some way injure the reputation of the person written about. Slight embarrassment is not usually cause for suit; but if the revelation would offend a reasonable person, it's likely actionable.

Also like libel, invasion of privacy can happen only to living persons. Dead people have no expectations, of privacy or anything else; nor can they be offended.

Unlike libel, though, violation of privacy deals with truth.

In an invasion of privacy suit, a court will give much deliberation to whether the disclosed facts are of public interest. Information the public has a right to know, or that is of interest to the public, cannot be considered private. Thus, a politician's affair may be disclosed; but publishing a story about a generally-unknown person's might bring the writer as much grief as her subject.

However, a case may still be brought against an author who discloses the politician's affair if the author intruded into the politician's secluded life, such as by using a drone to look into his windows or planting a spy-cam device on his property, to discover the facts of the affair. If a reasonable person would expect the information to remain confidential, an author should think well before divulging it.

Once the affair is made known, invasion of privacy is no longer actionable. Every writer in the country may publish what they know of it, because it's no longer a private fact.

An expectation of privacy exists only in private places. If the politician kissed his mistress at a ballgame, or even the public spaces of a hotel such as the lobby or hallway, he should not expect that to be kept secret. Disclosure of actions performed in public places do not generally infringe on the right to privacy.

Everyday Application

To use private parts of a person's life in your work, change enough details about him that readers won't recognize the model for the sleazy character in the book.

Publicity

Some things are meant to remain private; others are meant to shouted from the rooftops. Celebrities—meaning, in this case, people who make money from their name or likeness (famous people)—have the right to shout their own name and endorsements.

Does that mean a writer cannot write about a celebrity, or have a famous person appear in his book? Not necessarily. A writer can have his protagonist run into Trevor Noah at a soccer game or Jennifer Lopez at a restaurant (as long as he doesn't cast them in a disparaging light).

What the writer cannot do is use the person's fame to sell his book, or imply that the celebrity endorses it. (Thus some biographies are "unofficial"—the label gives notice that the personality does not endorse it.)

A famous person's name, image and likeness, and identifying characteristics are all part of his persona, and he is the only one who may use them for financial gain. No one else can take advantage of the luminary's status without permission.

This means no part of his persona may be used for any advertising, merchandising, endorsements, promotional, or commercial proposes without his permission.

Everyday Application

Putting a movie star's picture on a book cover, using a bestselling author's name in a fake endorsement or as a nom de plume, or naming a protagonist Taylor Swift are examples of things that take advantage of the celebrity's reputation. Doing so not only falsely implies connection to her, it also detracts from her own ability to use her fame, which is her livelihood.

Takeaway

In general, a writer may have celebrities appear in his book. But he should avoid:

- defaming her

- invading her privacy by revealing private facts or information about her; or

- taking advantage of her persona for his commercial benefit.

Thank you for reading!

I appreciate the time you've taken to do so.

If you found the information in this book helpful, please consider letting other writers know.

Some great ways to do this:

- Word of mouth—tell all the writers you know

- Leave a review on Amazon and/or Goodreads

- Rate other people's Amazon reviews as helpful

- Consider gifting a copy to your favorite writer(s)

- Post about it on your social media and blog

- Ask your library to order it

- Ask your local bookstore to carry it

Thank you for being a responsible writer
and a good literary citizen!

Where to Find More Information

As you can see, there is more to copyright than many people realize. Here are some resources for more information:

US Copyright Office
https://www.copyright.gov/
877-476–0778
The ultimate authority on copyright.

American Bar Association Intellectual Property Law Group
https://www.americanbar.org/groups/intellectual_property_law/
If you need an intellectual property attorney, you may want to search here to find one.

Dear Rich, An Intellectual Property Blog
http://dearrichblog.blogspot.com/
This blog contains a wealth of information on copyright. You may submit questions.

Project Gutenburg
https://www.gutenberg.org/
This website contains several volumes of indexes for copyright renewal registrations.

About the Author

Teresa Lynn is not attorney, and nothing contained herein is, or should be construed as, legal advice.

Teresa Lynn is a writer and editor with a background in journalism and education. She has written for a range of publications on a variety of topics, including book publishing, current events, historical topics, food, nature, and pop culture. She has authored three books, *Little Lodges on the Prairie: Freemasonry & Laura Ingalls Wilder, Thanksgiving Joy*, and *Understanding Copyright: Author's Edition* under her own name, as well as several ghostwritten works.

In 2014, Teresa helped establish Tranquility Press, a hybrid publishing company near Austin, Texas. Today, she provides all types of writing, editorial, and publishing services.

She is administrator and board member of Story Circle Network, editor for FOL-Georgetown, Vice President of ACFW-Cen-Tex, and Distribution Editor for Story Circle Book Reviewers.

In addition, she is a member of the Writers League of Texas, Women Writing the West, the Former Texas Rangers Association, the Order of the Eastern Star, and the Laura Ingalls Wilder Legacy and Research Association.

She speaks to groups nationwide on writing and publishing, Freemasonry, Laura Ingalls Wilder, and the Texas Rangers law enforcement agency.

In her free time, Teresa enjoys reading, traveling, and seeking out little-known history of interesting people and places. She lives in Georgetown, Texas with her husband, near their two grown daughters.

For more information on writing, editorial, or publishing services, or to arrange a speaking engagement, contact Teresa through any of the following:

email: tranquilitypress@gmail.com
website: www.henscratches.com/
blog: https://henscratches.wordpress.com/
Tranquility Press: http://tranquilitypress.com/

www.ingramcontent.com/pod-product-compliance
Lightning Source LLC
Chambersburg PA
CBHW071433210326
41597CB00020B/3776